Tiger Cub
by Monica Hughes

D1011942

Editorial consultant: Mitch Cronick

Copyright © **ticktock Entertainment Ltd 2006**
First published in Great Britain in 2006 by **ticktock Media Ltd.,**
Unit 2, Orchard Business Centre, North Farm Road, Tunbridge Wells, Kent TN2 3XF

We would like to thank: Shirley Bickler and Suzanne Baker

ISBN 1 86007 973 3 pbk
Printed in China

Picture credits
t=top, b=bottom, c=center, l-left, r=right, OFC= outside front cover
Alamy: 13, 24. Corbis: 4, 5, 16, 19, 20, 21. FLPA: 1, 10. Getty: 14.
Photolibrary (Oxford Scientific): 12, 15. Superstock: 6, 7, 8-9, 11, 17, 18.

Every effort has been made to trace the copyright holders, and we apologize in advance for any
unintentional omissions. We would be pleased to insert the appropriate acknowledgements in any
subsequent edition of this publication.

CONTENTS

What is a tiger?

A tiger is a big, wild cat.

Tigers live in forests and jungles in Asia.

Tiger

World map

Asia

Other big cats

Lion

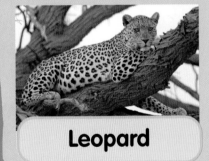

Leopard

Cheetah

What does a tiger look like?

This tiger has orange fur and black stripes.

This tiger has white fur and black stripes.

It has blue eyes.

All tigers have sharp claws and big teeth.

Teeth

Meet a tiger cub

This is a tiger cub.

The tiger cub lives with his mother.

The mother tiger has two cubs.

The cubs are brothers.

Tiger cub

The tiger cub cannot see when he is born.

Mother tiger

Tiger eyes

The tiger cub opens his eyes when he is about two weeks old.

At first his eyes are blue.

When he gets big, his eyes are yellow.

Looking after the cub

The mother washes the cub with her tongue.

She carries him in her mouth.

Tiger cub food

The tiger cub and his brother drink their mother's milk.

After about six months, they can eat deer and pigs.

Their mother catches deer and pigs.

She gives some of the meat to her cubs.

Hunting

The mother tiger takes the cubs hunting.

The cubs watch her jump on big animals.

The cubs play and jump on each other.

Then they jump on small animals.

Grown-up tiger

After two years the tiger cub lives on his own.

He scratches the trees to tell other tigers to keep away.

He roars if other tigers come near.

Tigers in danger

Tigers are in danger.

Some people shoot tigers to get their fur.

Some people cut down the trees in the forest.

Then the tigers do not
have a home.

Yes or no?
Talking about tigers

Tigers live in forests and jungles.

Yes or no?

A tiger cub is born with his eyes open.

Yes or no?

Tiger cubs stay with their mother when they get big.

Yes or no?

People kill tigers for their fur.

Yes or no?

All tigers look different.

What is a good name for this tiger?

Activities

What did you think of this book?

 Brilliant   **Good**   **OK**

Which page did you like best? Why?

• • • • • • • • • • • • • •

Which is the odd one out? Why?

cheetah • dog • lion • tiger

• • • • • • • • • • • • • •

Draw a big picture of a tiger and label it.
Use these words:

claws • stripes • teeth • tail

• • • • • • • • • • • • • •

Who is the author of this book?
Have you read *Orangutan Baby* by the same author?